Never Offer a Chair

to a Dancing Girl

By

Jamie Givens

authorHOUSE

1663 LIBERTY DRIVE, SUITE 200
BLOOMINGTON, INDIANA 47403
(800) 839-8640
www.authorhouse.com

© 2004 Jamie Givens.
All Rights Reserved.

No part of this book may be reproduced, stored in a retrieval system, or transmitted by any means without the written permission of the author.

First published by AuthorHouse 11/15/04

ISBN: 1-4184-8113-0 (e)
ISBN: 1-4184-8111-4 (sc)
ISBN: 1-4184-8112-2 (dj)

Library of Congress Control Number: 2004097802

Printed in the United States of America
Bloomington, Indiana

This book is printed on acid-free paper.

*For my first poetry teacher,
Ruby Givens (1911-1999).*

Thank you

First, I would like to thank Holly Waldrop and Julie Fesmire for the editing support. Thandi Murray and Curtis Rose for supplying Fresh Produce themes. Thanks to Ruby Green Gallery for supporting the poetry community in Nashville, Tennessee. Thanks to Dennis Wile for the great photos. Thanks to the Neuhoff Complex for the use of the Poet's Garden. I want to thank all of my friends and muses. Mostly, thank you Joe Richards for saying, "What do you have to lose?"

Table of Contents

If I Wrote a Poem 1
Super Sonic Addiction 3
The Cowboy 4
Horses 6
To Be Like You 8
Dancing Girl 9
Lightning Amen 10
Sensitive Ears 14
Did I See Him? 15
Sigh! 16

Who Was Watching Whom 19
When It Rains in the Desert, It Is Time to Cry 21
Now 22
Mono Speaks 23
The Week That Was 25
Susan World 27
Greeting the Fires in Me 28
Mono Moods 29
Gentle Rain 32
Apples 33
Once You Have a Barbecue 34
And Now for Something Completely Different 35

Grandpa Went to Cuba 39
The Day I Came of Age 41

    Charlie's Backyard 43

    Rites of Spring 44

    Untitled: 45

    If My Memory Were Erased… 46

    Electricity 47

    Haiku 48

    The Milk of Kindness 49

    The Price for Freedom 50

    Hold Me 51

    Fatalistic Attraction 52

    Grandpa Went to Cuba 53

Can You Swing **55**

    Where the Heart Is 57

    Probability Patterns 58

    Blood 61

    Susan World Changes 63

    Sustenance 64

    Matayo Darling 65

    Re-Generations 66

    Jazz Theory 67

    You Were Never Mine 68

    Shallow Jazz Roots 70

Fresh Produce **73**

    Fresh Produce: 75

    April 12, 2003 76

Harmony through Conflict 77
May 10, 2003 78
The Keys of We 79
June 14, 2003 80
Virion 81
July 12, 2003 84
Bodies Are Her Business 85
August 09, 2003 87
Course of Intuition 88
September 13, 2003 89
Autumn Desert Has No Leaves 90
October 11, 2003 91
Guilt 92
November 08, 2003 93
Can You Repeat That Please? 94
December 08, 2003 95
The Miraculous 96
Haiku 97
January 10, 2004 98
Revolution 99
February 14, 2004 101
When I Was Young 102
March 06, 2004 103
Trash Night 104

Mangos for Chutney **105**
   Still Life..107
   The Diver 108
   Where I Want to Die......................................109
   Ode to a Mango 110
   Lush Dream 114
   Juicy 116
   Haiku...117
   The Last Mango 118
   My Plan 119
   Breakfast...120
   Some Like It Hot 121
   Harvest..122
   Mangos for Chutney..123

If I Wrote a Poem

Super Sonic Addiction

Hello, my name is Jamie, and I am a Sonic-aholic. It all started in 1995 when I experimented with French Fries and Onion Rings. Soon, four times a week, 10:30 P.M., young pony-tailed blonde girls would bring me an order of little stuffed jalapeños, Ched-R-Peppers. One day my body had an intervention. My liver balked and gall bladder revolted. Nausea with its green-tinged hues tamed my wild desire for that hot fried food.

But, I couldn't stop from pulling into Sonic's trademark stalls. Grilled Cheese made with Texas Toast was my next great passion. I like it when the butter saturates the bread. Then, I moved on to Grilled Chicken with honey mustard. Sometimes I would order my secret obsession, Tatertots with Cheese. The day I bottomed out my order had been an Extra-Long Chili Cheese Coney, no onions, large Chili Cheese Fries, Old Fashioned Root Beer Float, and a Hot Fudge Cake Sundae. Later that day, I went back for a Frito Pie. I couldn't help it!

It was a super-sonic addiction. The only cure was to move from the franchise locations. Then I came to Tennessee, and all it took was one hot summer. We're talking Route 44 size Cherry Limeades, Oceanwater, Vanilla Malts, and Lemon Fresh-Fruit Slushes. As the humidity presses into my face, I'm not ready to give up these simple pleasures. My only hope is moderation, or maybe one day I can learn to drink sweet tea.

The Cowboy

The unassuming Stetson sat crooked on the Cowboy's head. He looked at me with one eye, then the other beneath the gray brim shadow. The maverick drank coffee and breathed in smoke from his hand-rolled cigarette. I could see the stories that lay buried beneath his weathered eyes. When he moved to town, the electric company went neglected. I wondered how many of those lines deepened by squinting in the dark. I wanted to pull from him the tales of life in the saddle. He wore a smile that old cowboys get after years of hard living, hard riding, and sharp shooting with the women.

After years of chasing mother cows and their scrawny little calves, he liked a slower life. Sometimes, he would work for free helping a neighbor, my dad in particular. He had a swift hand when it came to branding. An expert, he knew just how hot to get the iron, not liking to see the animals suffer. The secret was his quickness in motion, making sure not to linger. No one spoke of his talent. In the commotion, the gift went unnoticed.

In my youth, on a chilly November day, I worked with the men sorting cattle. I directed big ass bovine to the corral on the left, and the puny suckers to the right. We spent break time in the tack room with space heaters brought from home. As he shared the Black Velvet, the cowboy nudged the bottle in my direction. Sly and smooth, he passed the forbidden beverage my way. I took a swig. It was a mighty but painless blow. I felt like a yearling under the touch of his branding iron.

In his youth, this son of a pioneer started to carry a firearm, out of habit instead of show. The gun was small and had a handy fit. There's this story that he would never tell of a blistering hot July day in the hills looking for strays. He rode with a drug store cowboy whose new spurs chinked as they trotted. The sound grated on my old friend's nerves. He decided that he needed to have a little medicine to ease the tension. They came upon a mineshaft, and old boots swung out of scuffed stirrups. The elder waved the kid inside. Frozen eyes followed under protest abiding by the command. Beer was in there from last Spring. It sat in a pool of cold water. The cowpoke had a tradition of leaving a six-pack in nature's refrigeration. The unmistakable sound of a western diamondback's rattle filled the dug out cave. Suddenly, the cowboy pulled out his revolver. He shot only once, and then silence echoed in the blackness. A direct hit in the head killed the snake. It was then that the young man knew he was only an imposter of a dying breed of men.

The Cowboy and I sat in the red vinyl booth at the Lazy J Diner. I offered to pay for the plates of biscuits, ham, and eggs that covered the table. Out of honor for my family name, he refused the consideration. As he slid sidelong around the edge of the table, he growled at me to leave a damn good tip. At the register, he reached for a toothpick and laughed at something with our waitress named Betty. In that moment, I wondered if he ever got lonely. I could only guess if circumstances would leave me, in my golden years, alone. Then, once again, I watched his fast moves. He slipped a single arm around Betty's waist. With the grace of a dancer, he guided her in a two-step dance behind the counter and ended with a twirling dip. He kissed her cheek and tipped his hat. He smiled and said, "Darling, I'll see you later."

Walking ahead, I waited for him outside. When he reached the door, the cowboy had already gained back his rigid sandstone composure. As we walked to my pick-up, his eyes twinkled when he saw Granddad's old blue Ford. My eyes squinted into the eastern sun as I thanked him for breakfast. He moved the toothpick to the corner of his mouth, breathed a deep belly full of air. The cowboy smiled, winked, tipped his hat and said, "Darling, give my regards to your mother.

Horses

Have you ever seen a runaway
herd of mustangs? The wild horses
that dare humans to tame them.
Unshod hooves kick up bleached
adobe ground creating sounds
of a thunderous rumble that can

only be heard within a heart beat.
Unfettered, never knowing the taste
of a metal bit in the mouth or the feel
of a woven wool blanket thrown over
the back with anticipation of a saddle.
I have watched personalities filter

past the tribe. Two tall Spartans
rear on hind legs ready to do battle.
Snorts of greatness blow from flared
nostrils. Competition over control;
contention for herd dominance.
Wildness has always captivated me.

A free spirit racing is what I love.
My horse was wild and free,
domesticated only by barbed wire
and bales of hay. Never ridden,
and left unnamed. I had fantasies
of a rodeo horse, the bucking bronco

that cowboys could never ride.
Angered when the farrier cut
her mane. I wanted a mustang,
a horse that dared men to tame!
What happened? A small man
with a need to prove his bigness

attempted to break my horse.
What broke was her front leg
when she escaped the heaviness
clamped on her back. I arrived
home from school surprised,
my father was at the back porch.

He was shaking. I could not
tell if it was from the actions
of his hired man or because
he had to face me. I was angrier
that my Dad had no intentions
of firing the bravado man

that shot my horse.
All I could do was pray
to the angels to lead her
where the wild ones are.
Lead her to a place where
no one will dare to tame her.

To Be Like You

I want to be like you, and walk
with the gait of unshackled liberty,
taste the sweet hard candy of independence
as I travel on this wayward rim rock edge
and go a million motorcycle miles.

I want to be like you, and live
with a pond and swim in rain water.
Take tickets at Friday night football games.
Touch the lives of the hometown crowd.
Discover how to use the English language.

I want to be like you, and have
my easy rider youth again. Wrong turn
decisions before the yield sign could be
undone. Not have caution hitting the brakes
watching the high-speed chase of Southern life.

I want to be like you, and taste
full-bodied wisdom in my graying years.
Live past the hardwired fear grid of decent desires
over toasted and slightly burnt, made juicy with
pineapple marmalade and strong black coffee.

I want to be like you, and know
the intricate lace pattern of who I am in each
bare bottomless experience sought. The riches
and jewels of freedom are only a perception. Time
shared moments are encoded with options to choose.

Do I really want to be like you?

Dancing Girl

She dances among the trees,
and on the ground above
she does a dervish whirl.
She dances across the land
with nowhere to go. She

tap-danced into the hearts
of men. Soft-shoe shuffled
around the jealous women.
The jitterbug of her youth
carried a cowboy's love.

Married a bebop master,
a waltz that didn't last long,
then drug herself back home.
She danced alone in high tops,
took barefoot ballet steps

up a mountain. Red clay
squished between her toes
when she did the twist in mud.
She wants to learn the hula
and dance under island palms.

Too shy to be like Salome
and dance with seven veils.
Early one morning the music
made her move. She was told
to take a seat. In her defense

an elder spoke these words,
"You never offer a chair to a
dancing girl! Never, ever
offer a chair to a dancing girl,
she just might sit down."

Lightning Amen

What can I say about a man I never met?
After seven years of traveling with the
neo-nomad hippie caravans, I learned
that this man was a God to some people
that I have known. The first to come
forward was John the Apostle, and like
John the Baptist before him, he came out
of the desert with his message clear.
The headlights shone bright on my
Mazda GLC. John said he came to dim
them, but it was my inner light alone
he attempted to extinguish. We went
to the Salton Sea Market, I thought to
get beer. He witnessed to me about his
Lord, Amen. I was drunk when we
finished the twelve-pack. Apostle John
said that the Lord would be proud
that I had shared in communion with
His chosen.

John lived with Cockroach Connie
and her three girls in a blue converted
Crown bus. The Lord teaches forgiveness,
and this was the lesson given to Connie,
forgiveness of the Apostle John for
the burn scars she suffered when he threw
Bacardi 151 in her face as he waved a handful
of lit sparklers. The Lord Lightning Amen
said it was really Connie's fault. She was
to blame; she had already been marked
just by being a woman.

Two years later, out of the Anza-Borrego
desert, Ezekiel appeared. Lightning Amen

had christened the name. After several
swill quality beers, Ezekiel had a gift
of prophesy. He would fervently preach
to us the supremacy of the Lord Amen.
The pious pinnacle of Zeke's message
always caused me to smile when he would
spew forth the words, "I just hate people
who don't love Amen!"

Zeke explained to me the ways of his religion.
It was simple; the Lord cares for the Brothers,
the Brothers care for the Sisters, and it is
the Sister's job to take care of Lightning Amen
and His Sons. Lee Ann cared for Ezekiel
and their twins. She was not yet a devotee.
Lightning Amen had not accepted her.
Lee Ann had not proved herself worthy
of His praise gained by being tortured
with sex as a sacrifice unto Him. The last
time I saw Lee Ann, the fire had left her eyes.
With her head bent down, she explained
that her name was now Rachel.

Autumnal Equinox 1991, I camped with
the Rainbow family on Mount Shasta. We
gathered in Panther Meadows to celebrate
the Fall. I met a Rainbow sister there
who had no name. She did have five kids
in a dirty green Ford van with a husband
called Job. I thought, "Oh God, not
another one." Troubles weighed heavy
on Job's heart. The Lord Amen knew
this when He called this son into service.

No Name had taken her little ones and
fled Lightning's tribe. She harbored
with a family called Love. Job found her,

and now they were traveling together.
No Name felt vindicated for leaving
Amen. She was really the righteous one.
Lightning Amen was spending time
in jail for the possession of a controlled
substance, with the intent to sell.
Job corrected her story. He told me it was
really a set-up by a fascist government,
scared of the truth of the Lord Amen.

Months and miles later, I traveled to
New Mexico in search of adventure.
I crossed the swollen Gila River with
clothes clutched overhead to keep dry
from chest-deep water. I scaled red cliffs
meant only for the naturally selected
hooves of Rocky Mountain big horn sheep.
I was on my way to a hot springs
affectionately called Bubbles because of
the effervescent quality of water.

I thought I was alone when my naked
body dipped into the percolating pond.
It was like soaking in hot club soda.
I gave my thanks to the angels for the
gift of the source. Movement in the murky
pool focused my attention. A man's head
rose from the liquid surface. His hair
dripped wet, and his beard remained
dry. His eyes were closed when he
exclaimed to me, "Our Lord Jesus Christ
was released from prison today, Hallelujah!"
I smiled because I knew the story continued.
The Diaspora was over! It was a recall
on souls, this Brother Scott was on his
way to declare himself unto the service
of the Lord Lightning Amen.

Scott produced his plans for pilgrimage.
He only wanted one hundred bucks
for the 1976 orange short box Chevy.
I considered the purchase until I heard
my friend Chuck give his two-part
warning. First, Chuck asked me
consider any bonds that tied me to
Lightning Amen. The second omen
was one of function; the headlights
on the Chevy had shorted and worked
no more. I pondered the problems
when there is no light.

Two young men bought this last
possession, and Scott was free
to fulfill his life's mission. It has been
over ten years since I watched him walk
into the juniper and pinyon as an answer
to Lightning's call. I never knew where
the Lord called home, my guess was
southern Arizona. The vision I had
of his lair, a den of darkness. A place
where a scorpion sits, tail perched
ready to sting with lightning speed,
a shock that would knock your lights out,
Amen.

Sensitive Ears

Be careful, sensitive ears
are out there watching
for the dark words
spoken from life's

unpleasant shadows.
Averted eyes only listen
to content that lies on top
of a starched white carpet.

Lumps of unsuitable material
hide under the rug asking
to be heard by sensitive ears.
Intentions can be as good

as gold teeth, but the glimmer
shines as bright as fool's grade ore.
Who wrote the book of rules
that explains poetic discernment?

Where are the laws that tell me
what is safe or out of bounds
for such sensitive ears?
I thought Allen Ginsberg

went through censorship's fire.
The howler won the court battle
freeing the poet's virtue
protecting us from these

sensitive ears. The ones
that watch for dark words
spoken from life's
unpleasant shadows.

Did I See Him?

I thought he was looking for me
past the glass window filled with
Italian cooked mahi-mahi and
potato cakes slowly eaten, until…

I thought I saw him (!)
copper-fuzzed hair sprouting
under an oily cap, wearing
the enshrined tie-dyed shirt of blue,
hiding fiery muscles that once held me.

Didn't he burn that shirt (?) with his
welding torch of oxygen and acetylene
after the hours spent in a dentist's chair
filling eighteen gaping cavities, breathing
through three pain-struck root canals,
pulling all four of wisdom's teeth.

The faded blue security shirt
that smelled of ground down polished
enamel and the gas that made him laugh.
The tie-dyed shirt of blue with drops of
vermillion blood spilt from spitting lips.

Didn't he burn that shirt?(!)

The window's pain reflects
an empty plate heart hungry
for carrot-caked innocence
and soft-shelled boyish ways.

Before leaving, I look past
the wooden gate door.
In the pink sunset's glow,
I wait for him to wait for me,
but it wasn't Tim.

Sigh!

If I were to write a poem about you,
I might be inclined to expose our secrets
told behind the green closed door.
Explanations of the Southern dialect,
reservations about politics and life,
what you really think of the people that
took you out to dinner the night before.

If I wrote a poem about you,
discovered would be one secret.
The mystery of nights when sleep
is a chore and your head pounds,
here is the answer: you miss the solid
comfort of a wife long passed. Your
empty hand holding the stillness of dark.

As I write this poem about you,
I tramp back to the vault that stores bundled
melancholy, past the stacks of combines
and beans. Back to summer days I walked
with my own Grandfathers, when we worked
together as men in fields. Knowing without
spoken words, the love we shared.

I don't want to write a poem about you,
I don't want feelings that resonate with your own
family's tale. The story of your Granddaughter
going to college out of state and living apart from
all that she knows. Remembering when I left,
although it has been over twenty years,
I relive the hurt of saying goodbye once more.

I've done writ this poem about you,
after weeks of a pressured request.
Knowing it reads easier than
Longfellow's prose of Myles Standish
and Pricilla the Puritan Maid. Hoping
it is understood, if you hadn't of asked,
I would never have written a poem about you.

Who Was Watching Whom

When It Rains in the Desert, It Is Time to Cry

As teardrops of memory drench my soul,
heartache clears for another day.
What once was real has gone away, paths taken
on different roads. When it rains in the desert,
old wounds feel fresh. In the solitude,
the crescendo of heat compresses the isolation.

Animals hide in burrows preparing
for drenching water. The sky lights up.
Thunder quakes. The rain has come to share
moisture from heaven. Bushes bear the burden
of living to give shelter. Chaparral soaks up
the wetness to provide a shaded peace.
A reminder has been given, growth needs
water to sustain that which has been sown.

My tears come with the rain. Falling, they hit
the ground blending with the drops from above.
Tomorrow is a blue moon, yesterday I cried.
The rain does not stop, and my tears still flow.
Storm clouds tower, tortured emotions sink deep
in suspended separation. Once again, I am here.
Once again, I feel pain. Once again, I am alone.

Now

Walking on the space
between molecules
buzzing with atoms.
Revolving
electrons and protons
are the charges.
Being in the gap
of those
particulate matters
not for me,
but is the way
I know.

Accessing the moment
of eternity, perception
of energy moving,
vectors cross into oneness.
The vanishing point,
when outcome becomes
the horizon
of edgeless creation,
continuously manifesting.
Grace,
that is the gift
when we remember.

Mono Speaks

Listen.
The lake is talking.
She sings in the spring
as grebes come to rest
at her shore.
Gulls swing home
gliding on thermals.

When *Poconip*
fog rises,
Mono relaxes
her restraint.
She joyously
rumbles a song.
Wind raises
the volume
even higher.

The sun's
golden light
shines ice blue
over the lake.

Active waves
serenade
the morning dew
dropping on
the surface
of water.

Contrasts run deep
in this land of
black and white.

Still water whispers
the reflection
of tufa and Sierra
in this land
I have called home.

The Week That Was

I soak away the habitual
barbed-wire boredom
in a pressed-out galvanized
tub of wet vistas.
Water, soon to be tepid,

is laced with grapefruits,
dandelions, and juniper.
Hungry for a hummingbird's
portion of pink gazelle meat
intended for another turn

about time. I graze in an
orange poppy pasture
skimming with the wind
over bloody ground.
I play with a broken tattered

straw hat as it tumbles across
the dusty moon plain.
Caught on the edge
of a crumbling cornice
looking down on the

unloved stow-away
portion of me.
Tracing the jagged template
with an ultra-fine point of clay.
The face of wrinkled truth

bends a stoic arm, revealed
is a vanquished scarred heart
beginning to feel tactile
forgiveness for the first time.
Revolving doors of blithe

compassion stop half way
pushing me out into the empty
bleak street. The asphalt is lit
by fireflies and glowworms
hiding under pollywog toes.

I pay off the sultry perfumed
gatekeeper uncovering
encrypted power. Vials
of leashed resistance
live in a war-torn room

sprinkled with gun powder
stolen from the temple
of Red Dragons.
To become as one
is a forgotten worn out

denim dream hanging
from a broken down
line of clothes.
The uniform
of Wonder Woman

lies in viscous mud
permeated with the sweaty
stains of Sainted Martyrdom.
Only the Mother, Father,
and Lover trinity remember me.

Susan World

Controlled sanity in her life lies behind four baskets
full of laundry. Closed spaces ask for privacy,
a room she can call her own. The manufactured locks
her husband makes will suffice, until new doors arrive
to a house that is incomplete. Remembering when
her grandpa died, I met sister Jill, it was then I learned
of "Susan World". The siblings told me of a brother,
and his well-stocked bar in the trunk of a BMW.
How he broke the blender making Margaritas
on the bumper. I heard of cousins that showed up

in smelly, hard-core Confederate garb. The maps
they splayed on the buffet table were plans for
the next reenactment. She has three kids that
go to Christian school, raising the little ones right.
Softball nights are time well spent in dugouts,
coaching girls how to play the game in Susan World.
She has a dog, called Dolly, psoriasis has replaced
the hair. Front paws don't touch the ground, and it's
not the belly that drags. The name "Dolly" suits her.
The dog is psychotic, but psychologists do not exist

in Susan World. Everyone on the block knows her house
where there was a party. People brought filled plates
from home because there was no forewarning. That night
on July the Fourth, fireworks went off in the world of Susan.
I want to eat the deep fried turkey her husband makes
come November, and taste the beer butt chicken cooked on
the grill as summer's heat approaches. Susan keeps one
eye closed the other open to see when I infringe by speaking
about what life is like on the other side. Her hand goes up,
a signal for me to stop before I reach her walled boundaries
because I am much too wild for Susan's world.

Greeting the Fires in Me

The spinning wheel turns forming
a thread of light woven into a garment
serving as my vehicle to freedom.

Turning.
Turning.
Turning.

Samskara is the everlasting wheel of destiny.
Fire breathes on spinning light ribbons
of color connecting us to the vortex hub.

I wear this single thread cloak.
The pattern of cloth changes,
yet the thread remains the same.
Varied texture is weightless and free.
See through color is not transparent.
The cost of my covering is my life.
It fits only me.

Mono Moods

Sister Mono, Tufa Goddess,
her waves of gray bouncing
playfully to the stark-white
alkaline beach interrupted
by a black point of crushed
cinder. The basalt dome's
apex holds a secret waiting
to be found. Deep fissures
form small canyons where
earth has cracked from intense
heating. On the molten rock
wall, hangs a nest built by ravens.
Large twigs and small branches
expertly woven into a basket
that holds the young whose
talons are fully formed to size.
Beaks too large for downy
faces take food from parents
that look uneasily over their
backs at the intrusion. It is a
view seldom seen from above.

Negit is the dark volcanic
island cone named for the
wings of the blue-winged goose.
{modern folks call them gulls}
It is their nesting home.
A land bridge created by water
diverted from mountain streams
to the city south allows coyotes
to cross over and feast on
vulnerable chicks. *Paoha* is the
white island so named by natives
for the spirits that rise from
the mists of hot water and holes
of steam. The nature spirits now
play alone. This island beckons me
to visit, yet it is beyond my grasp
unless I paddle in a canoe.

Mono Lake is sweet to the eyes,
acrid in smell. Water I want to taste.
Water I cannot drink, more salty and
saline than an ocean. Only brine shrimp
swim under the surface. Brine flies born
in the water, crawl out to dry their wings
where they hover, never to fly around
a human. Sculptures of tufa rocks dot
the shore. Some stand as watchtowers
of another time. Some are huge stone
mushrooms. Rocks made by minerals
lain down by mixing fluids.

Shrouds of white ice ascend over the islands
at four o'clock in the morning. The *Poconip*,
a dense fog, swallows up the lake and
my small cabin. Three hours later,
the thickness of icy air has risen above
engulfing the town that sits on a mesa
overlooking Sister Mono. This morning,
as the sun rises, an orange sherbet glow
absorbs me. I watch two circles of multi-
colored sundogs playing on the water.

Winds blow over the crest of the Sierra.
Dust dances across the inland sea.
Water whips through the air.
Green turns the lake in spring.
Pink is the summer glow.
Yellow hues fade, as days grow short
into an icy blue cast of winter.
It is a place where all the colors
reflect Mono moods.

Gentle Rain

Facing the grey sky alone,
I wait for gentle rain to fall
against my face.

Fecund fields of sweet white clover
line the ditch bank memories of youth.
Swollen eyes pray for anvil-shaped
thunderclouds to come my way.

"Relieve me!" I plea.
"Please rain come and end the
tortured confines of monotony."

Row, after row, after row,
I cut hay with a sharp-toothed scythe.
Ravens swoop down, follow my direction.
The bird's black iridescence invites me
into the darkness alone waiting to discover
what is hidden in fallow plots left untended.

Apples

Granny smith apples
are all I see her eat
on Monday afternoons.
She tips her chin to the sun
as if to sing, "Hallelujah!"

Her tongue meets blush
apple skin; white teeth bite
whiter flesh. Juice drips
from her lips as she clamps
down on Eve's forbidden

food while lifting a basket
of laundry. When I watch
her, my mouth puckers for
tart pleasure. At the market,
my fingers trace bagged

Washington apples,
feel for ripe freshness,
cradle a red delicious.
Anticipation brings me
closer to the delicacy

experience, but a bite
of this hand-picked fruit
only leaves me hungrier
for a chance to eat a
granny smith apple.

Once You Have a Barbecue

Once you have sun-ripe peaches,
make a double crust pie.

Once you have a chest of ice,
stock it with Miller High Life Beer.

Once you have a cast iron skillet,
fry up hush puppies and catfish.

Once you have homegrown veggies,
create kabobs with wet bamboo.

Once you have red potatoes,
dice and cook for the salad.

Once you have coals white ash hot,
nestle in husk covered corn.

Once you have a blender,
froth up the Margaritas.

Once you have a plate in hand,
fill it with this home-cooked food.

Once you have dipped a spoonful,
chew slowly, savor, and swallow.

And Now for Something Completely Different
International Center for Gibbon Studies
Santa Clarita, California

A beautiful Fall day, a journey we took.
The wind was breezy.
The sun's rays cast long shadows.
The melodious songs the gibbons sang
rang out true. I thought they were asking
"Who the hell are you?"

The purple door that led
inside resonated peace.
The Goddess of Compassion
watched as the food was
reverently mixed by a girl,
quiet care for her primate friends.

Vocalizations
take me back
1984,
when I would sing
the gibbon's chorus
at a zoo
where I worked.

I felt envy of the young
watching them cling
to a mother's comfort.
Did I feel that closeness
as a child?
Is this a longing I have
because they are fuzzy?

Sharing a resonance
with a gibbon
called Cambio.
The eighteen year old
shares my mother's birth.
In the corner, far away,
is he shy or a loner.
We both wanted
the people to go.
We both longed
for the quietness
to come back.
Even I am too much.
The little one has hidden
from my view.

Repetition of movement.
Repetition of sound.
Are they bored?
Do gibbons know
contentment
playing a game.

Feeling the desert
Autumn sun,
imagining the feeling
of a cool forest floor.
Watching these creatures
brachiate as they radiate
across a canopy of trees.

Is rejection
of an offspring
rejection
of a culture
forced upon them
in captivity?
Would abandonment
occur in the jungle?

In the quiet spaces
we learn to be,
living and breathing.
I look to purpose.
My purpose,
our purpose,
as a species,
as a genus,
in a family,
called hominid.

The need
of eye contact,
what is the draw?
Ego-driven
communication
between the species?
Observer.
Witness.
Who was
watching whom?

Grandpa Went to Cuba

The Day I Came of Age

Coming home from an Indian summer vacation,
stopping at Wendy's to let my hot motor cool, I spied
a 1967 baby blue Volkswagen Beetle cherried out with
low-backed seats and sideboards rimmed with clean chrome.
She was a shiny sister to a bug I once drove. As my eyes
tracked that silver bumper, I felt lusty energy pump from
my lead foot revving up into my loin. I longed to drive that
baby blue back into my past memories of icy mountain
snows and visits with my old friend, Frank Chop.

Behind the wheel of that classic car sat a young teenage
hippie boy. Love beads hung below a beard that tried to
flourish on a face that looked like Jesus. He was the only
one of his caste in this small Georgia interstate town.
I saw him eye my out-of-state truck stocked with camping
gear, road map folded on the seat. I wanted to jump that
boy's baby blue VW, roll up the window, and go all the way
to *Mulege* on the coast of Baja California. We could say
he's my son to avoid suspicion of kidnapping a minor. He
could fish for sea bass everyday. He would be my model
as I painted his sun-browned body on a naked canvas.

A jagged cut from a B-grade movie flipped me forward
several years. I lived complacently in a travel trailer,
cropped gray hair topped my leathered face. The boy had
filled out into his manhood. His unhinged power played
pissed he spent these sacred years running on the *playa*,
keeping his body supple for a worn out artist going
nowhere.

I looked again at that boy and his blue VW. He knew I was an outsider; the driver to his highway dreams. I walked past my blown tire fantasy with hands close enough to touch the boy and his blue VW. I whispered to him, "Hey, I like your car." His eyes looked through me. He didn't even smile. My eyes, hot with scorn, turned away from the boy and his blue VW.

Charlie's Backyard

Travel on highway three-three-one, over
the Choctawatchee Bay, veer left then
south again, to the edge of Seagrove town,
behind a wall you will find Charlie's backyard
where red, yellow, blue, and white prayer flags
from Bhutan flap and fly a silent invocation.
Words of blessing accompany the ancient
winged Garuda creature that carried the teacher
of teachers. Buddha, the enlightened one,
waits with compassion. Lung Ta the wind
horse rides on with powerful primal fury.

Charlie's backyard languid stairs step
down to sand so pure and clean, grains
squeak under weight-bearing points on feet.
Sugar white sand the color of crustacean
crushed shells sifted to a confectioner's
consistency. In Charlie's backyard, Mexican
Gulf water surges to the bleached shore.
Past the breaks, at swell's crest, a single
pelican flies in symmetry above the fluxing
surface. Wherever low or high tide crashes,
time and space are obliterated.

Rites of Spring

Wrinkled coal black goddess reflects
the luster of a lip-licking blaze.
Her fierce muscular knees pump
upward brushing gold-encrusted ears.
Her silent trance voice calls me to join
her feverish effortless passion dance.

Maha Mata Kali,
your undulation of destruction
merges with infinite creation.
My corporal expression watches
the fires of regeneration peak higher.
Threat of incineration does not
stop the mother. She grows in
tandem with the burnish flame.

She entices me with wild wicked promises.
She unfurls the feast of celebration,
the orgy of disruption.
She is the one to ask Shiva to drum,
and dance a little faster.

Untitled:

I sit with dangerous deviant moods
by the satin grayling moss pond.

Early dawn, twilight hour
my body knows not
which one.

Complimented blessings
thrown away, heaped upon
accumulated littered shale.

Rocks
tinkle
crumble
clink
tumble
thunder
shunned
crash
anonymous.

Can it be
what Jim said is true?
"Depression is only unresolved joy."

If My Memory Were Erased...

Can I forget my mother
is it allowed,
forget the one that
birthed me.

Can I forget my father
his absence from family,
forget his late
night arrivals.

Can I forget the boys at school
ignorance went ignored,
forget their
grabbing hands.

Can I forget my lovers
heartaches untended,
forget how many
they number.

Can I forget the fool I've been
so many times before,
forget the embarrassment
of being unaware.

Can I forget the magic of life
a crystalline edge,
forget the honing that gives
me shape and form.

Can I forget who I would be
in a golden moment,
forget everything but
the gift of spontaneity.

Electricity

When Zen bathing
rises enjoyable sitting
listening to alternate
current one hundred ten.

Haiku

Plop darts of color
Individuality
Autumn leaves turning

The Milk of Kindness

Anke, you are asking me to slaughter all of my sacred cows! Not just the ones that are weak and thin, but you challenge me to kill the whole herd after years of rising every morning, early dawn, tending to my holy cows! With pounded copper buckets, I brought water drawn from the Springs of Knowledge. All the days spent combing ivory tresses with bristlecone brushes and lilac-scented water, teasing their tails into fluff-ball illusions cinched with mottled ribbons.

My docile darlings wear offerings of braided orange and yellow marigold harnesses. They domesticate in sacrosanct pastures. My sacred cows love to munch on oats mixed with molasses, the fodder filling fat and sassy bulls. Cowbells jingle and clankle as my blessed bovine graze in fecund understory. I have been so proud of my hallowed herd and their robust offspring.

Therefore, my friend, I have come to accept your harsh resolution. When sacred cows come to my attention, I will lead them to the Slaughter House of Denial's wide white doors to an assembly line of death. Hanging on hooks, carcasses suspend from well-lit ceilings. I will ask the butcher to cut pieces small enough for us to roast in your open pit flame.

The Price for Freedom

A ship comes in from China,
containers of cheap plastic goods
hide smuggled passengers
that lie in a week's long journey.
Suffocated from stench and lack of air,
they paid the price for freedom.

A train comes in from Mexico,
containers filled with paper products
easily made south of the border. Four
families from Guatemala, hidden from danger,
lay dead from desert heat overexposure.
They paid the price for freedom.

A wooden ship comes in from Africa,
containers lined with human cargo.
The Middle Passage made by 50-100 million.
Abduction, enslavement, journey across the
Atlantic. One-half died, never made it. Alone,
away from home, they paid the price for freedom.

Hold Me

Come to me my lover of eternal fires,
wrap me with bent elbows and knees.
Hold my head with your work-stained hands.
Cradle me with the strength of your full
blooded arms. Hold me until my body
merges with dust shards from borne out of
wedlock dreams. Hold me down to the count

of roses Mary offers praying hands fitted with
tired rosaries. Cover me with kisses as I lie under
the moonflower tree. Hold me to the ground
glinting with mica. Breathe into me the flame
of colored cloth worn by the ascended master.
Help me find the Earth Mother's home. Take my
body to her, eat her food of blue corn grown

on the canyon lands and mesas. Hold me to her
ground, be willing to stay until she says, "Let go".
Hold me until I am small and weak like a child
after walking first steps. Hold me until I am
fed with the bread of devotion, until my lips
touch the chalice filled from the fountain of life.
Hold me until I fall asleep.

Fatalistic Attraction

Addicted to
the thrill
of passion
lovers invent
wispy words
creating
a mood.

Flirtatious eyes
invite a kiss
lashes lower
to something more.
Boldness seduces
unwavering meek.
Cat and mouse
games have
set rules.

No, I mean yes!
Yes, I said no!
Maybe, just this once.
Who is the prey
when mouse
catches cat?

Hiding secrets
from the world
lovers play
their games.
Fantasies indulge
addictions of
passionate thrills
where being caught
is the score.

Grandpa Went to Cuba

Grandpa went to Cuba.
The Idaho farm boy was
only twenty when he
strutted the high seas
and wore a navy uniform.

Grandpa went to Cuba.
Havana was a gambling hamlet.
People lived with poverty rules.
It was before the revolution,
no one had heard of Che Guevara.

Grandpa went to Cuba.
Cruiser docked he came on shore.
The trained tough soldier softened.
Smiling, he sat on a tile porch
and joked with children.

Grandpa went to Cuba.
A wooden box of family photos
kept the memory recorded
by Grandma's pen. Her blue
ink handwriting told the secret.

Grandpa went to Cuba.
A fact not known or I would
have asked about the picture
taken of him sitting on stairs
talking with two boys from Cuba.

Can You Swing

Where the Heart Is
for Matisse

Icarus was the first modern jazz dancer
when he listened to his father and strapped
on wings made of beeswax and feathers.
Minos, Knossos palace king, commissioned
architect Daedalus, planner of the labyrinth pit.
After completion, the ruler sentenced the builder
forever to live in a tower with his son Icarus.

Able to escape with a ladder, the two gathered
seagull down splayed out smaller to greater
on a wooden frame. By air was their only savior
fleeing the island of Crete. Watching the weather
potential moisture dampens the armature,
elder cautioned younger not to fly over the sea.
Another possible danger, navigating too close

for Helios, God in the sky. Parlaying pure
joyous movement, Icarus' improvisation jammed.
Exalted soaring glory, riding thermal wind waves,
he flew like an osprey in spring. Forgetting
vulnerability, not following father, the child's
heartfelt folly and creation beauty moved
his taught body loosely like Ben Vereen.

Loosing focus in his dance of flight, golden
warm light rays softened beeswax holding
grey-white seagull feathers tight. The offspring
of Daedalus plunged into the bay ending his
dance of plight. Icarus was the first modern
jazz dancer when he listened to his father
and strapped on hand-made wings of might.

Probability Patterns Written While Watching the Movie, Mindwalk

Electrons show up
only when quantifying
potentiality of reality.
Extruding circumlocution,
probability patterns are
predictably measured
like photons traveling at
constant speeds of light.

Probability's pattern of
interconnection resounds
in Nature's essence.
Matter reaches out
to form harmony relations.
Objects interface in
approximation chords.
Cosmic ray delivered
particles bombard the
poet's dance connecting
the stabilizing chaos
of our fishing village.

Probability patterns
drive the force of
haphazard randomity.
Creates accountability,
misshapen responsibility.
The one who pays decides
fascination and value, but
doesn't ask the solution
question, lost in an
oversize picture book
projection, compounded
by eminent domain.

Proof provided concrete
packaging wrapped in
symbiotic seasonal change.
Living the system of
recognition, probability
patterns spin silhouette
outlines of self-organized
cellular maintenance renewal.

Template stability
most assuredly has
inherent inspiration
to transcend avoiding
the corrupt obsessive
pursuit of growth.
Reaching for the brass
ring fastened into
happiness, the longed
for object thought to be
gained after longevity,
sustaining probability.

Compromising water
negotiating soil
over uneven Earth.
Mediation of erosion
equals the sum of longing
added to metaphors
of oneness. Solidity
perpetuates the eternal
paradigm prediction.
The intention that
our universe needs
to be healed of its
primary infection:
the notion that
big bang separation
is the original sin.

Blood

At 41
I am bleeding,
bleeding inside
taste the blood
in my mouth
rising from
a cast iron skillet.

At 41
I am bleeding,
bleeding inside
chills from winter
isolate a fevered
punch-drunk
afternoon sun.

At 41
I am bleeding,
bleeding inside
locate wounds
bathe constantly
utter small words
guttural sounds.

At 41
I am bleeding,
bleeding inside
proper courage
harsh wisdom
gentle ivory
soap cleansing.

At 41
I am bleeding,
bleeding inside
taste the blood
in my mouth
bleeding inside
I am blood.

Susan World Changes

Muddy red brick, manicured mortar walls
cracked the foundation that contained Susan
World, the day her husband said divorce.

The husband grills the beer butt chicken.
The husband fries the Thanksgiving turkey.
The husband coaches softball in the spring.

Cape fear red painted walls closed close around
warped pergo flooring, the kitchen buckling
under the weight of Susan World crumbling.

The husband she stood behind nineteen years.
The husband cannot keep a business open.
The husband created a cemetery plot of debt.

Youngest daughter, now nine, wears ivory pajamas
splattered with green leaves and red cherries. How
will Susan tell her after Christmas, they are moving.

The husband now sleeps alone.
The husband shouts, "Get out!"
The husband Susan still loves.

Sustenance

Breathe slow take a bath imagine a lover whose
wholeness of spirit envelopes a body and water.

Breathe slow like a full moon red in mourning
floating across trees whose leaves rustle in silence.

Breathe slow let me pull you into my belly.
Breathe slow let me meet your heart.

Breathe slow let me be your inspiration,
exaltation, aum, and salutations.

Breathe slow as the blood in my veins
pulses to the rhythm of your…

Breathe slow open to the expansion.
Breathe slow surrender into the contraction.

Breathe slow beat the drum, play, hum,
shake, shudder, quake, have tremulous fun.

Breathe slow dive deep and leave
fingerprints on the floor of my ocean.

Matayo Darling

Impermanence is loss anticipated.
Resistance to life reduces self-expression,
and growth implies decay. Are you

committed to outcome of effective
perfection undiluted by pretension, left
flawless without snagged judgment?

Severe limitations line up like braided boxed
thoughts labeled, "Inhaled Rationalizations".
Sit on the maven's shelf and hear the secret:

to answer the mystery is not important.
Clowns weep for less as they dance
around puddles of spilled red makeup.

Re-Generations

Mother, a honed lioness
reigns the jungle tinder.
She is a firefighter.

Sister, a sleek swan feather
cruises through open water.
She is a Coast Guard Captain.

Grandma, a granite cistern
holds life-giving fluid.
She is a pediatrician.

Daughter, a pearl iridescence
passes her first driver's test.
She is a woman.

Jazz Theory

I'm a minor chord
waiting to be played,
drinking red wine
rolling on my tongue
like a diminished G seventh.

Altering an interval
for a Monday interlude,
but the tri-tone I'm blowing
is too sharp for augmentation,
no need talking to a plastic surgeon.

Just searching for a taste
of F flat on the treble staff,
think I'll go down on
the bass clef for a while.

Baby, I'm a minor chord
waiting to be played
on your fretless strings,
liking the way your fingers
linger on the root scale degree.

You Were Never Mine

The afternoon sun hid from nimbus
clouds. The savior's voice swallowed
hard as plums and cherries were eaten
by hard-luck youth destroyed by past
patterns of blue and green shame.

Po' Boy Sandwich Shop only serves
the rich with fancy tiers of masterful
guilt laid down the speckled rock shore.
Halogen lit minefield circuit's cut short.

Don't you see me here, next to you?
Don't you want me here, next to you?
Don't you hear me, next to you?

Subtext Salute: "The American Beauty"
Is it her waves of grain caressing the
developed, barbed wire plain where
spun-honey girls dance and wiggle?
Clothes come off one strap by one lick,
teasing us with saliva wet fingers.

Power is in the pussy!
Power is in the pear-shaped ass!
Power is in the possessing!

No one cares if you take a peek as
substitute summers fill in for the real
affair, when we were so sure of what we
wanted against the backdrop of tension.
Now I don't know what I want, or what
your millions can afford. Can dreams be
bought at discount from the Dollar General?

Will you continue to take notice of shallow faces and plastic size double D's? Will you continue to blame the witches and snares for your lack of position? Will you swim with me in the salty night sea, across layers of froth and foam and traverse the Indian Sub-Continent? Or will we move into the gloom of too many marriages, too many children, and too many marvelous lusty leisures? You, my lover, were never mine.

Shallow Jazz Roots

"Jazz oboist is an oxymoron,"
scolded the purist. I had heard
about this cat from Oregon,
he was playing fusion. But,
the voice of jazz reason anointed
my head with a worn neck strap
attached to the high school's
used tenor saxophone. My fingers
went from trilling F sharp on a
baroque chart penned by Joseph Haydn
to popping mother of pearl pads
playing *Stuck on You*. Not to mention
a more important lesson: the proper
tonguing technique on the chorus
of *Night Train*. My lips went from
the embouchure of a dainty, delicate,
double reed to a thicker, rounder,

fill-up-your-mouthpiece grip that
men commented about later.
My first day at the university, the jazz
instructor asked, "Hey baby, do you
swing?" Induction into the band came
with the admission, "Yeah, I know how
to play." That impatient conductor
suffered the aftermath of not asking
the follow-up question, "How well?"
I don't know if it was innocence or
ignorance when through the cacophony
of a college cocktail party I queried
Clark Terry, "Which instrument do you
play?" Sadly, I learned the truth from
the master himself, Dizzy Gillespie
when he refused to baptize me.
With a blessed Baha`i bebop bellow,

he bent over and bammed me with,
"Jazz musicians, they can play classical!
Classical musicians cannot play jazz!"
His wisdom put a damper on my
endeavor to practice the tenor. But one
voice remained that kept calling me,
"Listen to my refrain, the name's Coltrane."
Nearly twenty-one, the month July,
I switched off the stagnant summer
swelter and stepped into the Record
Exchange. Flipping disks and reading
between liner notes, there he was...
Coltrane. The album, it read *Coltrane*.
I could listen to the man, he only cost
a dollar. The owner that sat behind
the glass counter looked up from
his newspaper and smiled. In my

basement apartment, lights dimmed,
I proceeded with ritual inspection
and cleaned the vinyl. The LP slid
on the Magnavox stereo my parents
bought when I was five. As the album
dropped, I brushed the needle and sat
back with a juice glass full of red screw-
top wine listening to the sax legend
John Coltrane. This is Coltrane?!
Can I give you my first impression?
He played like a steam *loco* motor
on the tracks packed with black coal!
Ready to burn, he was in position
for an improvisation. In the confusion
of horn blowing notes bending and
swerving, he was headed for a collision!
Somehow, he pulled out at the very end.

Fresh Produce

Fresh Produce:

Fresh Produce was a twelve-month, live, thematic poetic experience sponsored by Armonia Nashville and Ruby Green Gallery.

Starting April 2003, a team of poets was selected to serve as "Fresh Produce" poets for a one-year period. Participants were challenged to be disciplined, prolific, and step out of any comfort zones by writing on a pre-selected theme in a seven-day period.

All of the writings "freshly harvested" at the end of the week were read at Ruby Green Gallery. Fresh Produce offered original, first-run, never heard before poetry. The following twelve poems are from this experience. The themes have also been included.

April 12, 2003

When you see the theme, you may immediately think of a song title. You may think of the late, great pianist, Bill Evans – side man/co-writer to one of jazz's greatest stars, Miles Davis. You may think of jazz, the art form...the outlet. Your thoughts may roam to the piano, itself, or Evan's classically trained, jazz-inspired mastery of it. You may even think of war, destruction...or- on an opposite notion...peace. Perhaps you will think of what peace means to you. Maybe a quick mind game of word association will leave you pondering inner peace, world peace, peace and quiet, war & peace...pieces of dreams?

Where do you find your peace?
What is your personal definition of peace?
Have you ever found it? Do you seek it?
Have you ever even looked it up in the dictionary?

April's Theme:

"Peace Piece"

Thandi Murray

Harmony through Conflict

The cone of a sleeping volcano,
clouds of dust settling after
the Earth stops quaking,
pea-green sky clearing
from a whirling wind,
boats bouncing in a slip,
peace smells like lapis-blue
lupine blooming a year
since the forest burned.

New mother wincing from a kick
to the ribs in her third trimester,
curvature of my soft palate
when swallowing a sip of beer
and my mouth answers, "AH!"
brakes screeching with the silence
of a non-impact succeeding, peace
sounds like the life force leaving
a body gasping its last breath.

May 10, 2003

This month's theme is simple. But, there is a new twist...

The May 2003 Fresh Produce theme is

"We"

There are two simple rules:

1. *Your poem cannot include the words "I", "me", "my", or "poetry".*
2. *No profanity.*

Thandi Murray

The Keys of We

We stand like twins and triplets.
We serve as raised guideposts
and solitary planks. Transposing
language, we speak with consistent
scaled overtones. Coexisting
together, we are black and white.

We siblings share jigsaw cut
spaces. Our wooden row homes
are upright, spinet, and grand.
Emory polished ivory skins and
ebony curves strike, hammers
hit wire. We sing in octaves,

twelve tone voices leapfrog jump
over pitches and invert, repeating
the melodies from Western world
music. Babies pound open-palmed
patty cake as youngsters plunk
us in practice. We long for a caress

in concert. We tinkle and thrum
arpeggio board games. In unison
or in consort, we wait to be touched
by artist's hands. We come to fingers
that stroke and push us. We are keys
of joy to the one who plays us.

June 14, 2003

*Will you think of computers, SARS, the common cold,
or love when you ponder this month's theme?*

*You may have one on your computer.
The world is trying to stop one is its tracks...
and some say that love is one.*

This month's theme is

"VIRUS"

Thandi Murray

Virion
Director of Human Resource
VFW Headquarters
Suite 13 Mumps Building
212 Rubella Way
Interferon, Ca 93705

June 20, 2003

Open letter to the Human Race

Dear Homo Sapiens,

First, let me introduce myself. My name is Virion a thirty-nanometer polio particle and Director of Human Resource for the Viral Federation Worldwide. The VFW would like to take this opportunity to apologize for any transmission attacks, blight, plagues, pestilence, endemic epidemics, corrosive corruption, infected lesions, rot, scourge, and contagious contaminations caused by members of our organization. We do not mean to be the bane of civilization. We have affection for your species. We also feel that it is important that your race understand our case. Humans and viruses alike procreate. Mea Culpa for maladies suffered, but we have to live somewhere.

While it is true, we create to replicate, viral infections also agreed to dissipate. Smallpox is just one example. This pandemic had its last stand. However, the humans have continued to hold the final DNA strands. West Nile Virus was meant to be contained in a distinct location, but birds migrate. We are not to be blamed. Foot and Mouth Disease was a practical joke that got out of hand. Ebola was a huge mistake not intended for Africans. Moreover, we must admit the infection of the eye named Coxsackie was supposed to go lower. As far as the problem with Yellow Fever, please stay out of the jungle because we have to live somewhere. SARS is a covert operation. The biggest mystery is HIV. Our Internal Affairs is leading the investigation. We are trying to get to the very bottom. We asked for Hepatitis A and B to turn in their resignation. They countered the offer with strain C. Frankly, between you and me, I am embarrassed by the Herpes blister from simplex to zoster.

Regarding viral complaints in agriculture, I have interesting information. Tobacco Necrosis, Ring Spot, and Vein Mottling are sponsored by the American Cancer Society. Hop Latent virus activity increased during prohibition. The VFW suspects the DEA is behind the Sunn-Hemp Mosaic misery in Pennsylvania.

Now, I would like to illuminate your kind about our family. The VFW does not recognize computer viruses since malicious men manufacture them. Epstein-Barr is not a virus. We have no record of it on our roster. Retrovirus causes tumorous cancer, not melancholy for disco music. Toad to human contact does not cause Papilloma warts. Although we have to brood somewhere, virus granules are not free living. We are imprisoned within the walls of a cell, not the seat of a toilet. Antibiotics will not kill us since we renegotiated our contract. When the union went on strike, vaccines were made with scab labor.

Finally, I would like to address the emergent virus future. It is contingent on Human behavior. Social events, hospital care, public health infrastructure, food production, and deforestation effect adaptation and viral production.
Yes it is true, virus particles mutate due to YOU! Please remember, we have to live somewhere.

On behalf of the Virus Federation Worldwide, thank you for your time and the consideration of our plight. For further solicitation, contact me at 1-888-4smutch.

Sincerely,
Virion

V:jzg

July 12, 2003

July Theme:

Ah! The wonder of the Human body! It is usually in the summer that we give more thought to our bodies – but usually because we're trying to find the perfect swimsuit with which to compliment/showcase/camouflage/tuck it, whatever the case may be. But our bodies are our shelter, transportation, raiment, warehouses, engines….and as we age, in our frustration with
the process we may think of them as our prisons. When the body, for reasons of age, disease, misuse, or overuse, ceased to work in the way were accustomed, we tend to forget what a marvelous machine it is. So, to give us all a little reminder and inspiration, let's all look at today's theme...

"Job 10:11"

No, this month's theme is not a religious or biblical one – unless you want it to be. It is all about the body. It just so happens that this month's theme provides an excellent description of its wonder. How would you describe the human body? Its wonders, its woes...dimensions, capabilities? No, you don't have to use Job 10:11 in your poem, just use it as an inspiration point
for describing this "contraption we came in." Have fun and hurry...you only have seven days.

Thandi Murray

Bodies Are Her Business

Glowing dim as a white star
from a far-away haven,
human body come to a table
made with birch, maple, and
leather. It is the workbench
of the Master's handmaiden
sent to polish the dust from
your tetrahedron light. Come
to the inner decompression
chamber, it is there you can
breathe a little wider and be
anointed with fragrant oil.

Human being wound taught
as a copper wire, the hand-
maiden is a body worker
here to serve you a favor.
Heat from hands register
like a steam radiator, ridges
on fingers meet firm skin.
And then, she moves through
you like a warm knife cutting
cold churned butter. Superficial
to deep, tracing muscles, tendons,
and bones she plucks fibers just

as a harpist plays a Celtic tune.
In this dance together, steps move
toward the nonlinear time zone.
Curves of flesh are familiar terrain.
Dissolving glue, she unwraps stuck
wax paper from saltwater-taffy-like
musculature and unwinds the pain.
Penetrating down to the red marrow,
she makes contact between the etheric
and physical. Human bodies come accept
the open invitation and receive healing
from the Master's hand-picked maiden.

August 09, 2003

You may have had a sneaking suspicion about this one...

The August Fresh Produce theme is:

"Intuition"

Thandi Murray

Course of Intuition

Dark and cloudy, lost driving
on an unknown byway, how
do I find the direction north?
When ruby throat hummingbirds
beat wings, speed counts two
hundred times per second, do
they have an inkling their flight
is south? Is it the same instinctual
intention that takes porcupine
caribou through a migratory loop

leading to Arctic tundra calving
grounds? A flash of insight, one
may reason, reveals knowing
I don't like someone, yet not
knowing why. Is it a sudden
inspirational voting booth
epiphany that casts a name
on the ballot in a school board
election after moving to a new
location? How about the hunch

playing red twenty-two as
the roulette wheel spins. Is this
the same foreseeing when playing
a number on the company employee
Super Bowl football pool? Is it direct
innate perception that shows which
path of faith is the correct reflection
to believe in? Do we listen for
the Buddha of Wisdom and follow
a course of intuition? Or, do we ignore
smelling the Holy Spirit's breath.

September 13, 2003

*It is a month, a song, a time in and of our lives...
and in 2001, it became eternally connected
to the infamy of a pivotal day in American History.*

This month's theme is simply

"September"

Thandi Murray

Autumn Desert Has No Leaves

Alfalfa has been cut third time this year,
scanty hay bales dot barbed wire fields
forgotten until potato harvest ends.
Trucks with ten wheels drive through deep
rich sandy loam, home to Luther Burbank's
russet spuds dug by a John Deere.

Bluebird school bus yellow and black
idles, stop sign flapped out, lights flash,
diesel fumes spew as children board.
Pom-poms shake, bleachers filled with
families, the pigskin flies through the air
and popcorn is sold by sophomore girls.

Ford Broncos and Jeep Wagoneers sit
at Fish and Game checkpoints. Men sport
unshaven faces that smell of blood, buckshot,
and beer as they produce their license to kill.
September the month I was born, Dad rode his
Honda motorcycle and Mom turned eighteen.

October 11, 2003

Who is to blame for what? Which man/woman/child/country precipitated which crime/argument/conflict at which moment in time? Who should apologize? Who are the victims? Whose face has the power to launch a thousand troops/missiles/ships? Whose version of which story will win the fight/case/cause? Once the truths are revealed, what will become of innocence?

This month's theme is....

"Guilt"

Thandi Murray

Guilt

Gravity heavy
gravity heavy
pulling out to in
rushing to cover
fresh-made tracks.

Gravity heavy
gravity heavy
pushing tombstones
over dirt-filled graves
mourners left behind.

Gravity heavy
gravity heavy
wealth adds weight
controlled only by
diet spending sprees.

Gravity heavy
gravity heavy
duty to parents
relationships carry
extra responsibility.

Gravity heavy
gravity heavy
saturated grey wool
coat hangs on
a burdened heart.

November 08, 2003

Turn it on its side and it becomes the symbol for the mathematical concept of infinity...

Biblically, it represents "new beginnings"...

Historically, it represents the number of lashes issued for chastisement during Roman rule...

All other numbers can be formed from part of it...

*Are you getting the picture? Here is a hint...
How many months have we been hosting
"Fresh Produce"?*

Here is another hint...list the parts of speech...if you add them, you will come up with this month's theme...

"Eight"

Thandi Murray

Can You Repeat That Please?

Eight, eight, eight,
what did you say?

Eight, eight, eight,
are you sure?

Eight, eight, eight,
what can I do?

Eight, eight, eight,
next year my boy is nine.

Eight, eight, eight,
Doctor's words a blur.

Eight, eight, eight,
what do they know?

Eight, eight, eight,
ovarian cancer, stage four!

Eight, eight, eight,
more months to live.

December 08, 2003

Theme for December
Fresh Produce is:

"The Miraculous"

I have experienced
Miraculous
happenings in my life,
and I imagine you have as well.
December
brings a season
of remembrance of such things
close to many hearts,
but I expect to hear
many other perspectives
of the
Miraculous.

Curtis Rose

The Miraculous

Miraculous miracle whip
sweet, tangy, and smooth
mixed in potato salad.
Wet spread cushions
tomato, turkey, Swiss
on rye. My mouth filled
with deviled egg ways.
So much tastier than your
bland cousin mayonnaise.

Haiku

Poets write alone
An everyday occurrence
The Miraculous

January 10, 2004

Wouldn't it be tedious if the January theme were Resolution?

I thought so too – but in keeping with the notion of change...

The January 2004 theme is...

"REVOLUTION"

Have fun!

Thandi Murray

Revolution

Spin of a
bicycle wheel
sings,
"Whirrrr!"
Follow one
single spoke
spinning,
tuned to sin.
Singing
whrrrrr-
whrrrrr-
rrrrr-ing
hypnotizing.
Whirrrr-ring

decades pass,
backward spin
hypnotized seeing.
Spinning jenny
bringing change,
lessening labor
with each counter-
clock-wise turn.
Wheel of change
changing life,
industrial age's
spinning wheel.
Turning wheels
turning wood.

Donkey cart
wood wheels
(ageless) pulling.
Neolithic Sumer
pull toward
modern Babylon.
Grist mill tower
revolving-
grinding mill
workers working
pulverizing meal.
Circles press
on circles
pressing on

ancient circles.
Gathering hands
clasping together
shaping a clasped
circle dance.
Hands press on
hands pressing
encircling hands.
Entwined fingers
reach wide,
creating one
single revolution,
humans spinning
around tribal fire.

February 14, 2004

Happy Valentine's Day, everyone!

Certainly hope you don't think that this month's theme would be dictated by "cupidology". Actually, this month will be dictated by our surroundings. Fresh Produce will be inspired by the works of Didi Dunphy.

Didi's exhibition, titled, "Ollie, Ollie, Oxen Free" will help us rekindle our youth in a very tangible way...getting the idea? Well, let's all wear our tennis shoes so that we can explore art as social play...AFTER we (we, meaning you, of course!) read our poems – all of which must begin with the following line...

"In my childhood..."

Thandi Murray

When I Was Young

In my childhood, sputnik had circled
the globe. The country was war-torn cold.
Children were told to duck and cover,
protection from the heat of incineration,
and the fall-out from nuclear winter.

A Dallas motorcade ended with assassination,
a pall of grief covered citizens. The remedy was
Johnson's Great Society. Chained dogs unleashed,
gnashed teeth tore at congregations. On a motel
balcony, they shot a King. Bathrooms desegregated.

Hippies danced in the Summer of Love.
From above, napalm dropped on Viet Nam.
Disenfranchised soldiers came home stoned.
Alan Shepard hit golf balls while on the moon.
The Age of Aquarius dawned a sexual revolution.

Stained with the smoke from burning bras,
women's hands left smudges on glass ceilings.
Watergate described corruption, and cover-up
became a noun. I went to a school, built round,
and learned how to spell the word innocence.

March 06, 2004

Hello everyone,

Theme:

"Last But Not Least"

Thandi Murray

Trash Night

Leftovers, ten days old,
A roast beef sandwich dried out.
Swiss cheese can stay.
Tomato is rotting soft.

Bread baked two weeks ago has grown mold
Until trash night,
Then, I clean out the fridge.

Nuts are O.K.
Orange juice, how long has this been open?
Turkey breast is a little dried out...

Leave it, I will make a casserole.
Everything is getting checked,
Apples and peaches.
Sauerkraut that Joe made yesterday,
That gets thrown out too.

Mangos for Chutney

Still Life

Smell of ripe fruit
captures my attention
and leads me to
the scent of origin,
a wooden ringed bowl
sitting on a dining table.

Two black-spotted
yellow bananas cuddle
a granny smith apple,
but buried beneath
this living still life
hides one lovely mango.

The Diver

Bliss told me
her favorite place
to eat mangos is Fiji,

standing in Ono Island
waters, overlooking
the Great Astrolabe Coral Reef.

When the drops of mango juice
fall into the South Pacific Ocean,
she dives in after them.

Where I Want to Die

I know where I want to die.
Where midnight explodes
over dark water.
Where balled ocean
meets bald ocean.
Where sediment melts
like a milk chocolate
and cream confluence.

I know where I want to die.
Where sky escapes winter
palm trees grow in silver.
Where sand dunes are dotted
with crimson flowers.
Where painted rock caverns
succumb to pressure
birthing hot spring water.

I know where I want to die.
Where the ghat line starts
on the Ganges river.
Where saffron clad scribes
chew drupe fruit tree flowers.
Where mango bud nectar
infuses ink with sugar,
coating the words of a poet.

Ode to a Mango

Your skins,
I am told
are inedible.
Yet, having
tried the
evergreen covering
one encounters
when waiting
to eat a mango,
I embark
on a tasteful
journey
across the sea
to a grove of trees.

Who owns
the land
this fruit
calls home?
Who has the
daily ritual
of watching
and tending
the orchard?
What birds
rest in
sturdy branches.
Are there any nests?
How much water
is needed to fill
roots that spread out,
roots that dive deep,
roots that tap into
the belly of the
Earth Mother.

Evolution has
determined if bark
is smooth or scaly.
My hands envision
an opportunity
to touch the
outer covering
and reach
for offspring.
How do open
buds smell,
or is the
fragrance
hidden from
senses
like a ship
in the fog
searching
for a mooring
away from
rocky danger.

Keep looking
for a sign
of safety
nestled
in the arms of
branches
supporting
a home.
How are the
flowers colored
or do they only
come in white?

Celestial pollination
with flies of
different species,
occasionally visited
by a bee
because you
are so sweet.

Fruits of my
desires hang
ripe for the picking,
ripe for the eating,
ripe for the twilight breezes,
and bats flying.
How does
the trunk
hold up
in monsoon
weather or
tolerate
a drought?

Whose hands
picked these
lovely mangos
was it a
woman
or a
child?
Wooden crate
containers,
ships, trucks,
and trains,

how many
more hands
have lain
on these
mangos
in the bowl,
from the market,
to my house,
handling
with gentle care.

No bruises on
these mangos
touched by the moon,
touched by the sun.
What stars
have watched
these mangos grow?
How many
windy days were
celebrated with
golden festivals
on peaks
of mountains
and valleys below?

Oh my mango,
it is time to
bless you
before I
scoop out
your flesh
with a spoon,
and eat your
sacred offering.

Lush Dream

A sun shadow follows me,
below the turnpike, changing lanes.

Capturing a glancing blow,
diabolical delight of ice cream

enchants my mouth.
Following a windblown shirt,

gravediggers wipe sweat from brows
heavy with tension.

Increments of intensity crowd
jaded palaces of delightful women.

Kindred souls gather to serve in
languid afternoons tasting persimmons.

Mangos and guavas fill juicy lipped mouths.
Noontime is mellow for the jeweled encased home.

One tortured with continual pity,
pride of the master inside

quibbles about being disturbed.
Right good perfect and correct

stays inside the middle grounds.
Turn ahead - turn below,

"Understand nothing!" chants the groomed crowd.
Velvet shades pulled down in my palace home.

Windows closed off from the view within
Xanadu, the utopic scene of escape.

Yellow-haired goddesses sing of grace,
Zion is here.

Juicy

MA ◊ MA ◊ MA ◊ MA
MAN~N~N~N~N~N~N
GO-baby-GO-baby-GO
Man-oh-Man–oh-Man
Goooeeesss

Haiku

Green unripe mangos
Rest in a bowl at the store
I will not buy them

The Last Mango

From the hidden box
of favorite fruit,
I pick the ripest mango.
A careful cut with the
utility knife, the first third
slips from my fingers.

Pausing for a moment,
remembering the last mango
eaten over dessert at breakfast
or was it between long lovemaking
moments? I compared your juicy fruit
slicing to my own mango carving ways.

The second third of fruit
slips from my fingers,
my hand full of the final third.
Thick pulp surrounds
the seed pod, I bite
stringy flesh that clings
just the way you bit into
our last mango eaten.

My Plan

Another mango you share with me over
breakfast coffee and true German dark chocolate.
Once again you part a perfectly ripe fruit,
your fingers covered in sweet succulent mango ooze.

My mouth fills with anticipatory saliva
as a fantasy fills my head with fancies
of fruitful folly. After the knife has been
set down, I will hold your palm to my lips,
suck the sweetness from your fingers,
and search for my own musky tastes of pleasure.
One more slice of the knife and I will move closer…

Startled out of my plan
of action when with a towel,
you wiped your hands
after the second telephone ring.

Breakfast

In bed by your side
listening to the rain
thinking about coffee,
mangos, and more. But,

you offered hot cereal!
Oh my mango madness
reels, once more missing
moist fruit this morning.

Your special oatmeal mixed
with raisins, covered in cornmeal,
stirred with a teaspoon of honey,
and smiles. This tastes like something
I would make on a rainy midday morning.

Some Like It Hot

Lavender towel dries droplets
of water from my body.
Standing in the kitchen,
looking at the apple green clock
reminds me you left an hour ago.
Mango skins on the counter
are the breakfast refuse,
miel de mango puddles on the
cutting board. I look at the coffee
cup signed Vincent, and ponder
if van Gogh ever painted a mango
perhaps in his café still life, or was it
his friend Gauguin when he painted
exotic women with oil on canvas.

As if seeking nourishment from
a trip through the Gobi desert
I reach for the mango leftovers.
My tongue and teeth separate
the pulp from skin. The next piece
I devour even faster slowing down
as the pile lessened. Sinking
my lips into the flesh and kissing
the strips of fruit the way I really
want to kiss you. The final slice is
one to savor, however this last taste
of mango sat on the spot where I had
earlier cut a serrano chili.

Harvest

Mango season is over,
harvest is done. Leftovers
are on the ground for the
birds, ants, and rodents
to feast or store.

Prices in the markets soar
past unearthly rates.
Mangos are never sold
by the pound, but by the
solitary fruit. Purchases limited

to less than three, ripeness has a
small window of opportunity,
peak season firmness, succulent,
and juicy.   Knowing how to pick a
magnificent mango is the secret to life.

Mangos for Chutney

Looking for mangos, I'm making chutney.
Recipe calls for six, slightly green.
At the market, mangos were on sale,
two for a dollar. I was tempted
to write one more poem.

Sampling treats at the smoothie counter,
a cherub-cheeked man smiled. He handed
me a thumb-sized plastic cup, his voice
a sweet tenor, "Try this one, it is mango."
Bushy gray eyebrows lifted me into
a temptation to write one more poem.

While out socializing, I had a conversation
with another person about how much
she loves mangos. Everyone at the table
nodded in agreement. I was tempted
to tell the secret of one more poem.

There was a suggestion to write twelve poems
about mangos and arrange them in a calendar.
The feeling was familiar; it was like the time
I was walking at Radnor Lake, watching turtles
flop into water. Tempted to join them,
but I never took the bait.

In this book of poetry, the empty last page
called out, "Give in to temptation and finalize
completion. Please fill me with mango love
words." I could not bring this study to closure
until Karen tempted me with a basket filled
with Gillian's ripe southern peaches.

About the Author

Jamie Givens grew up on her family's ranch in Owyhee County, Idaho. In second grade, she placed second in a talent contest reciting, "I Know an Old Lady Who Swallowed a Fly". She attended Gonzaga University, Boise State University, and the New Mexico Academy of Healing Arts. She has traveled back roads throughout the western United States searching for hot springs and quiet spots. Jamie has lived in Germany, Washington, California, Alaska, and New Mexico. Givens currently lives in Nashville, Tennessee where she hosts poetry readings and has featured on local radio, television, art galleries, fundraisers, and the Southern Festival of Books. She placed second in the *Nashville Scene* 2003 poetry contest. She is a board member of Ruby Green Art Gallery.